MEASURE

Ivan Bulloch

Consultants
Wendy and David Clemson

2	What Size Is It?
4	How Tall Are You?
6	Puppet Play
10	Finger Puppets
12	Cut-Out Mask
16	Paper Dolls
18	Bottle Band
20	Mobile
22	Baking Cookies
24	Cookie Boxes
26	Wrapping Boxes
28	Sand Timer
30	Tangrams
32	Skills Index

A **TWO-CAN** BOOK
published by
THOMSON LEARNING
New York

2 What Size Is It?

Every day we ask questions such as:
How big is it? How tall is it?
How heavy is it?
What time is it?
All of these questions
have something to
do with measuring.
In this book we will
be looking at lots of
different ways of
measuring.

We use words such as big and small,
tall and short, or heavy and light to
describe things around us.

MAY

Look at the groups of objects on these pages. Which is the biggest in each group? Which is the smallest? Which is in the middle?

4 How Tall Are You?

Make your own height chart so that you can measure yourself.

● Stick several lengths of colored paper together to make one long strip that is taller than you.

● Use a building block as a guide to measure lines at equal distances apart down the side of the paper.

Colored Strips

● Use a ruler and the block to make strips of colored paper. The strips should be the width of your chart and the height of your block.

● Cut the strips out carefully.

● Stick one strip along the bottom of your height chart. Leave a space and stick another strip above the first one, using the lines you have drawn as a guide. Keep on sticking strips down in this way until you reach the top.

Here's what you learn:
● how to make and use measurement.

● Hang the chart on a wall so that the bottom touches the floor.

● Stand next to it and ask someone to make a mark on the chart right over your head. Count the number of strips from the floor up to the mark. Now measure your friends against your chart. Who is the tallest? Who is the shortest?

● Measure yourself and your friends again in one month. Has anyone grown taller?

6 Puppet Play

How big is your hand? Here is a way to make a hand puppet that will fit you like a glove!

Make a Pattern

● Put one of your hands flat on a piece of felt. Draw a mitten shape slightly larger than your hand on the felt.

● Cut out two mitten shapes exactly the same size. You could use different colors for the back and front.

● Place one felt shape on top of the other. Ask an adult to help you sew around the edge. Use brightly colored thread to sew the pieces together.

● Now you are ready to decorate your puppet. Can you guess what these puppets are going to be? Turn the page to find out.

Here's what you learn:
● how to investigate area.
● how to compare sizes.
● how to match shapes.

Here are the finished puppets! Just by adding a few bits and pieces you can turn your puppets into real characters. You can buy eyes to stick on, or make your own from pieces of felt. Ears, noses, mouths, and tusks can also be cut from felt and glued in place. Why not invent your own puppet?

Frog
Use green felt to make a frog puppet. Then give it a wide, red mouth.

Monster
Cover your mitten with spots to make a funny monster puppet.

Elephant

Use gray felt to make ears and a trunk for an elephant. Then add a pair of tusks to finish it off.

Shape Face

Make a face using squares for eyes, a triangle for the nose, and a long, thin rectangle for the mouth.
This puppet looks a little like a robot!

10 Finger Puppets

Here is an easy way to make a puppet that will fit on your finger.

Bird

● Cut out a small paper circle. Make a cut from the edge into the center.
● Fold the paper around to make a cone and tape the edge.
● Tape the cone onto the paper tube.
● Cover the paper tube and cone with several layers of paste and pieces of torn newspaper. You can make your own paste by gradually mixing water and flour until the mixture is thick and creamy.

Making a Tube

● Take a long strip of paper or thin cardboard and wrap it very tightly around your finger.
● Tape the end and then gently pull the tube off your finger.

● When your puppet is dry you can paint it. Why not make a puppet to fit every finger!

Sombrero

● Make a tube that fits your finger, as you did before.

● To make the sombrero, cut out a paper circle. Ask an adult to help you make some small slits in the center of the circle. Push the circle over the paper tube to make the brim of the hat.

● Cover the tube and brim with newspaper and paste as before.

Here's what you learn:
● how to follow instructions.
● how to investigate size.

12 Cutout Mask

We used a paper plate to make our mask. You will need to know where to make holes for your eyes, nose, and mouth. Here is a good way to take the measurements.

Measure It Out

● To measure the distance between your eyes, hold a piece of yarn in front of your face, stretching from the middle of one eye to the middle of the other. Then, lay the yarn in the middle of your mask and mark each end.

● Next, measure the length of your nose. Stretch a piece of yarn from the middle of your eyes to the bottom of your nose. Make a mark on the mask as before.

● Finally, stretch a piece of yarn from the bottom of your nose to the middle of your mouth and mark it on the mask.

● Make a small hole on either side of your mask, just below the eye holes. Thread a piece of yarn or string through each hole and make a knot in the end so that it cannot pull through. Tie the mask around your head.

Making the Mask

● Ask an adult to help you cut holes where you have marked the eyes and mouth.

● You can cut a hole for your nose, or make a flap by leaving one edge attached to the mask.

Once you know how to make a basic mask, you can make up all sorts of different ways to decorate it.

Tiger
● First, paint a striped tiger face on your mask.

● Next, cut out some paper ears, paint them, and stick them to the top of the mask.

Bird

The feathers on this bird mask are made from paper. Cut feathers in different sizes.

Glue the large feathers on first and the smaller ones on top. You can make the beak by folding a piece of cardboard and gluing it in place.

Here's what you learn:
● how to use measurements.

16 Paper Dolls

Here is a way to make a cardboard doll and a whole wardrobe full of paper clothes. First, draw the outline of a person on cardboard, or trace around the doll below. Ask an adult to help you cut it out. Then, make some clothes…

Making a Shirt

● Place the doll on colored paper and draw around the top half of the body.

● Lift the doll off and draw a shirt shape slightly larger than the doll's body.

● Draw some tabs on the top of the shirt at the shoulders. Ask an adult to help you cut it out. Put the shirt on the doll and bend the tabs over to hold it in place.

Making a Hat
● Draw a hat shape a little bigger than the doll's head.
● Ask an adult to cut a slit in the hat like the one shown below. Push the doll's head through the slit.

Here's what you learn:
● how to match sizes and shapes.
● how to investigate area.

Making Pants
● Place the doll on a different color of paper and draw around the bottom half of it.
● Lift the doll off and draw a pair of pants slightly larger than the doll's legs. Add some tabs at either side of the waist.

18 Bottle Band

It is hard to believe, but you really can make your own band with some empty glass bottles, water, a metal spoon, and a beaker to use for measuring.

● Make a mark about a quarter of the way up an empty plastic beaker.
● Fill the beaker with water up to the mark. We added a little food coloring to the water to brighten up our bottle band.
● Pour the water from the beaker into the first bottle. You may need a pitcher or a funnel to help.

● Pour two measures from the beaker into the second bottle.

● Now pour three measures into the third bottle, four into the fourth bottle, and five into the fifth bottle.

● Play your bottle band by knocking gently on the sides of the bottles with a metal spoon.

20 Mobile

This colorful mobile looks great hanging up, but the trick is to make it balance!

Cardboard Cutouts

● Cut out some shapes from cardboard. You could trace around the ones on this page, or make up your own.

● Decorate both sides of the shapes.

● Ask an adult to make a hole in the top of each shape and thread a piece of string through it. To make this easier, use a sewing needle with a large eye.

● You can also decorate balls to hang on your mobile. We used Styrofoam balls that you can buy in craft stores. They are very light and it is easy to thread string through them with a sewing needle.

Hang It Up
 Attach a piece of string to the middle of a long stick or piece of dowel.

● Tie the objects to the stick in different places. Once you have done this, you will have to slide them along the stick until the mobile balances. You may also have to adjust the lengths of the strings.

Here's what you learn:
● about weight and balance.

22 Baking Cookies

It's very important to measure carefully when you are baking. Ask an adult to help you measure out the right amount of each ingredient.

You Will Need:
3/4 cup all purpose flour
1/4 cup granulated sugar
1/3 cup butter
2 drops vanilla extract

● Ask an adult to heat the oven to 325°F.

Mix It Up

● Put the flour and sugar into a mixing bowl.

● Cut the butter into small pieces and add it to the bowl. Use your fingertips to rub the butter into the flour. (Make sure your hands are clean!)

● When the mixture looks like fine bread crumbs, add the vanilla extract. Use your hands to make the mixture into a large dough ball.

Roll It Out

● Knead the dough on a surface sprinkled with flour.

● When it is smooth, use a rolling pin to roll it into a thin, flat shape that is about the same thickness as a coin.

● Cut shapes using a cookie cutter.

● Put the cookies on a greased cookie sheet and bake them for 20 minutes.

● Ask an adult to take the cookies out of the oven. Use a spatula to put the cookies on a wire rack to cool.

Here's what you learn:
● how to follow instructions.
● how to use standard measures.

24 Cookie Boxes

When you have made your cookies, you might want to give some away as a present. Here are two ways of making boxes in which to pack them.

Pile Them Up
● Put one of the cookies on a piece of cardboard. Using a ruler, draw a square slightly bigger than the cookie. Cut out two squares exactly the same size. These will be the top and bottom of the box.

● Decide how many cookies you want to give away and pile them up. Stand a piece of cardboard against the pile to measure the height. Make a mark on the cardboard.
● Use a ruler to draw a cardboard rectangle slightly taller than the pile of cookies and the same width as the square you have already cut out. Cut four rectangles exactly the same size. These will be the sides of the box.
● Tape together the bottom and sides. Put the cookies in the box and tape the last square on to make the lid.

Spread Them Out

● Lay six cookies flat on a piece of cardboard and draw a rectangle around them. Cut out two rectangles the same size.

● Cut four thin strips of cardboard the same length as each edge of the rectangle.

● Tape the strips to the rectangle to make the sides of the box.

● Tape the other rectangle on one side to make the lid.

Here's what you learn:
● about area and volume.

26 Wrapping Boxes

Make some paper to wrap around your box by painting some plain paper.

Paint and Paper
● First, choose a piece of paper that will be big enough to cover the box.
● Splatter some paint onto the paper using a brush, or dab it on with a sponge dipped in paint.

Wrap It Up
● When the paint is dry, lay it with the decorated side down and place the box in the middle of it. Fold the long sides of the paper around the box.

● Wrap the paper around the box so that the ends overlap. Tape down the ends.

● Fold down the flap of paper at the top of one of the short ends. Then, fold in the two sides. Next, fold up the bottom flap and tape it in place.

● Fold the paper on the other short end the same way.
  You could decorate the box with a colored ribbon.

Here's what you learn:
● how to estimate area.

28 Sand Timer

Here's a way to measure how much time something takes.

Paper Cone
● Draw a big circle on a piece of stiff paper. You could trace around a big plate.

● Cut out the circle. Then, ask an adult to help you cut a slit from the edge of the circle to the center.

Here's what you learn:
● how to measure time.

● Fold one side of the slit around the other to form a cone shape, like this. Tape it in place.

● Cut a tiny hole in the bottom of the cone.

A Line of Triangles

Cut out some matching paper triangles and glue them in a line up the side of an empty bottle.

Falling Sand

● Place the cone in the top of the bottle and fill it with sand. Watch the sand fall through the cone and fill up the bottle. The sand gradually reaches each triangle mark.

● Have a friend watch the timer while you hop around the room. How many marks does the sand pass? Does your friend take the same amount of time to hop? What else can you time?

30 Tangrams

A tangram is a square that has been cut into seven special pieces. The pieces can be put together to make different patterns or pictures. Look at the pictures here. Can you find a small square and five triangles in each picture? The black shape is called a parallelogram. It is also in all of the pictures.

Making a Tangram

● Ask an adult to cut out a square from thick cardboard.

● Use a ruler and pencil to mark out the shapes in the picture.

● Cut along the lines and paint each piece a different color.

How many pieces make up the tangram? Mix them all up. How many pieces can you count now?

Use your tangram pieces to make a dog shape like this one. Can you see the dog's ear? Can you find its tail? Have all the tangram pieces been used to make the dog shape?

You can make all sorts of pictures with your tangram pieces. Try making a person running, like this one, or a bird like the one below. Then, try making your own pictures. You must use all the tangram pieces in each picture.

Back Together Again
When you have finished, mix all the pieces up again, then try to make the square.

Here's what you learn:
● how to investigate area.
● how to create pictures using shapes.

Skills Index

create pictures using shapes 30-31

estimate area 25-26

follow instructions 10-11, 22-23

investigate area 6-7, 16-17, 30-31
investigate area and volume 24-25
investigate size 7, 20-21
investigate weight and balance 20-21

match sizes and shapes 16-17
match shapes 7
measure time 28-29
measure using units 4, 18-19

use measurements 4, 12-15
use standard measures 22-23

Editor: Diane James
Editorial Assistant: Jacqueline McCann
Design: Beth Aves
Photography: Toby
Text: Claire Watts

First published in the United States in 1994 by
Thomson Learning
115 Fifth Avenue
New York, NY10003

Published simultaneously in Great Britain
by Two-Can Publishing Ltd.
Copyright © Two-Can Publishing Ltd, 1994

Printed and bound in Hong Kong

Library of Congress Cataloging-in-Publication Data applied for.

Consultants
Wendy and David Clemson
are experienced teachers and
researchers. They have written
many successful books on
mathematics.